Lerner SPORTS

MEET LAMAR JACKSON

PERCY LEED

Lerner Publications ◆ Minneapolis

Copyright © 2025 by Lerner Publishing Group, Inc.

All rights reserved. International copyright secured. No part of this book may be reproduced, stored in a retrieval system, or transmitted in any form or by any means—electronic, mechanical, photocopying, recording, or otherwise—without the prior written permission of Lerner Publishing Group, Inc., except for the inclusion of brief quotations in an acknowledged review.

Lerner Publications Company
An imprint of Lerner Publishing Group, Inc.
241 First Avenue North
Minneapolis, MN 55401 USA

For reading levels and more information, look up this title at www.lernerbooks.com.

Main body text set in Aptifer Slab LT Pro. Typeface provided by Linotype AG.

Editor: Annie Zheng

Library of Congress Cataloging-in-Publication Data

Names: Leed, Percy, 1968– author.
Title: Meet Lamar Jackson : Baltimore Ravens superstar / Percy Leed.
Description: Minneapolis : Lerner Publications, 2025. | Series: Lerner sports. Sports VIPs | Includes bibliographical references and index. | Audience: Ages 7–11 | Audience: Grades 4–6 | Summary: "Lamar Jackson is a two-time NFL MVP winner. With accurate passes, strong leadership, and record-breaking rushing stats, the Baltimore Ravens quarterback is one of the best. Readers learn more about his life and career"— Provided by publisher.
Identifiers: LCCN 2024022905 (print) | LCCN 2024022906 (ebook) | ISBN 9798765649251 (library binding) | ISBN 9798765662458 (paperback) | ISBN 9798765658512 (epub)
Subjects: LCSH: Jackson, Lamar, 1997-—Juvenile literature. | Quarterbacks (Football)—United States—Biography—Juvenile literature. | Baltimore Ravens (Football team)—Juvenile literature.
Classification: LCC GV939.J29 L44 2025 (print) | LCC GV939.J29 (ebook) | DDC 796.332092 [B]—dc23/eng/20240530

LC record available at https://lccn.loc.gov/2024022905
LC ebook record available at https://lccn.loc.gov/2024022906

Manufactured in the United States of America
1-1011065-53537-8/8/2024

TABLE OF CONTENTS

GOLDEN CHANCE 4
FAST FACTS 5

CHAPTER 1
NATURAL-BORN PASSER 8

CHAPTER 2
STARTING QUARTERBACK 14

CHAPTER 3
ALMOST PERFECT 18

CHAPTER 4
MAKING HISTORY 22

LAMAR JACKSON CAREER STATS 28
GLOSSARY 29
SOURCE NOTES 30
LEARN MORE 31
INDEX 32

GOLDEN CHANCE

Baltimore Ravens quarterback Lamar Jackson had the ball. Detroit Lions players rushed in. As Jackson's teammates held them back, he scanned the field. All he needed was an open player to throw the ball to.

With nobody in sight, Jackson ran behind the line of scrimmage. Two Lions players chased after him. Jackson kept his eyes wide open, waiting for his shot.

A golden chance showed up in Ravens player Nelson Agholor. He was in perfect position next to the end zone to catch Jackson's pass. Jackson made the throw. Touchdown!

FAST FACTS

DATE OF BIRTH: January 7, 1997
POSITION: quarterback
LEAGUE: National Football League (NFL)

PROFESSIONAL HIGHLIGHTS: was chosen in the first round of the 2018 NFL Draft; led Baltimore to the best record in the NFL in 2019; earned NFL Most Valuable Player (MVP) awards in 2019 and 2023

PERSONAL HIGHLIGHTS: grew up in southern Florida; won the 2016 Heisman Trophy; became the highest-paid NFL player in 2023

Jackson throws a touchdown pass against the Detroit Lions.

The Ravens destroyed the Lions in their game on October 22, 2023. Baltimore took the lead when Jackson scored a touchdown. They bumped the score to 14–0 when Jackson made a brilliant pass to Agholor near the end zone. The Ravens put up three more touchdowns by the fourth quarter. The game ended 38–6.

None of it would have been possible without Lamar Jackson. He is one of the best quarterbacks in the NFL. He can run and pass, making him a dual threat. But although he already has two NFL MVP awards under his belt, Jackson's goal is still to win the Super Bowl.

Jackson (*right*) and Agholor (*left*) celebrating a touchdown against the Detroit Lions on October 22, 2023

CHAPTER 1

NATURAL-BORN PASSER

Lamar Jackson grew up in Pompano Beach, Florida, with his brother and two sisters. Southern Florida is a hotbed for football players. But as a young kid, Lamar didn't care much about the sport.

In 2005, when Lamar was eight years old, his father had a heart attack and died. Lamar's mother, Felicia Jones, became a single parent to her four children. She did everything for them, from shopping to playing tackle football in the yard.

Lamar and his mother celebrate after he won the 2016 Heisman Trophy. The Heisman goes to college football's top player.

That year Jones enrolled Lamar in a youth football league. At first, he wasn't excited about playing. But he was the fastest player on the field, and he liked scoring touchdowns.

Lamar grew to love playing quarterback. With his mother supporting and pushing him, he worked to get better. In high school, he became the star quarterback at Boynton Beach Community High School. His skill drew attention from top college coaches around the country.

Lamar had enough talent to play college football, but some coaches weren't sure what position he should play.

Lamar runs with the ball during a high school football practice.

Lamar throws the ball in his first college game on September 5, 2015.

They thought he was a better runner than a thrower. Some teams even thought he should play defense.

Lamar wanted to play quarterback. Bobby Petrino, then the head football coach at the University of Louisville, told the family that Lamar would play only quarterback for his team. That was good enough for Lamar. In 2015, he joined the Louisville Cardinals.

Petrino kept his promise. As a freshman, Jackson played 12 games as quarterback. Then, in 2016, he had one of the best seasons in college football history. He threw 30 touchdowns and rushed for 1,571 yards.

That year Jackson won the Heisman Trophy as the best player in college football. He was the youngest Heisman winner ever. "I'm extremely proud to represent this class and the University of Louisville with their first Heisman Trophy," he said.

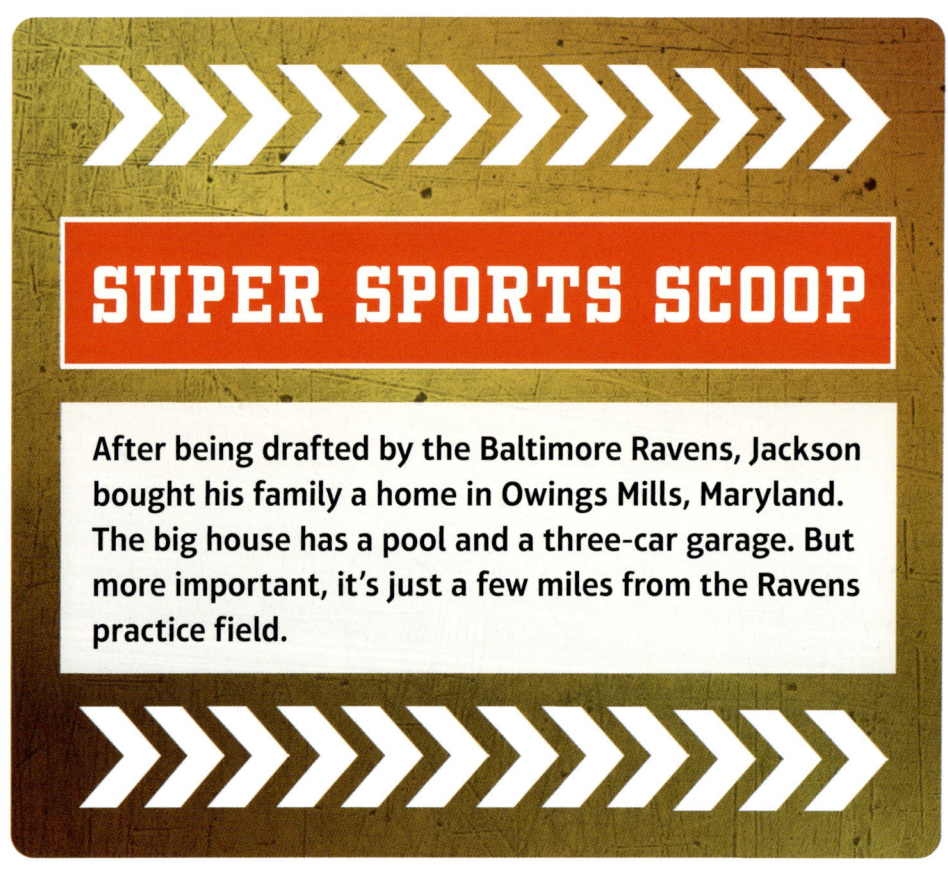

SUPER SPORTS SCOOP

After being drafted by the Baltimore Ravens, Jackson bought his family a home in Owings Mills, Maryland. The big house has a pool and a three-car garage. But more important, it's just a few miles from the Ravens practice field.

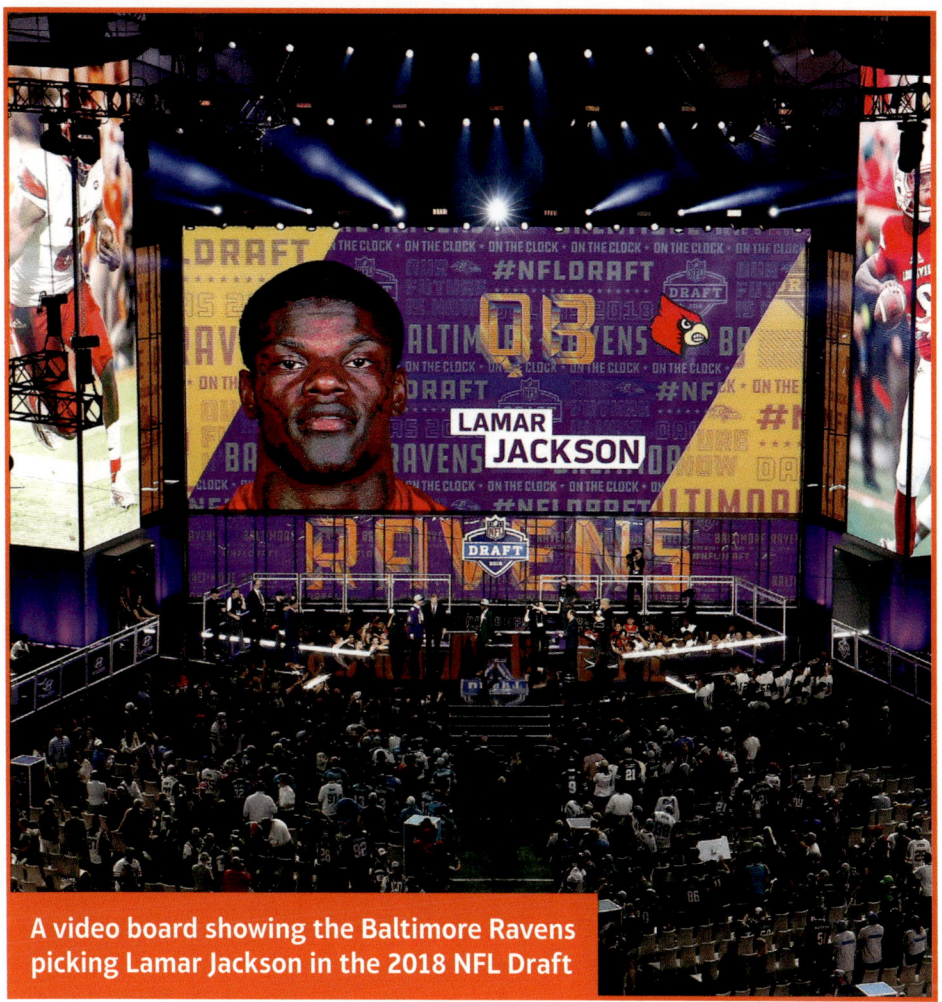

A video board showing the Baltimore Ravens picking Lamar Jackson in the 2018 NFL Draft

After his junior season, Jackson felt ready to move on and entered the 2018 NFL Draft. But some football experts still thought Jackson was a better runner than a passer. He waited as teams chose other quarterbacks. Finally, with the last pick in the first round of the draft, Baltimore chose Jackson.

CHAPTER 2

STARTING QUARTERBACK

When Jackson joined the Ravens in 2018, he became the backup to starting quarterback Joe Flacco. Flacco had been the team's starter since 2008. In 2013, he won the Super Bowl MVP award.

Ravens coaches were happy with Flacco. But in a game in November 2018, Flacco hurt his hip. Jackson took over, and the team won three of the next four games. When Flacco was healthy again about a month later, the coaches kept Jackson in the game.

Jackson scores a touchdown in a November 2018 game against the Oakland Raiders.

In 2019, Jackson was the starter from the beginning of the season. Defenders had no answer for his running and passing attack. In a December game against the Cleveland Browns, Jackson racked up 341 combined yards. He became the first player in NFL history with at least 3,000 passing yards and 1,000 rushing yards in a season.

It was a great year for Jackson. He won his first NFL MVP award, and Baltimore won 14 games, the most in the NFL. He was also voted to his first Pro Bowl and First-Team All-Pro teams. But in Baltimore's first playoff

SUPER SPORTS SCOOP

Jackson was the starting quarterback at the 2020 Pro Bowl in Orlando, Florida. He was the youngest quarterback to start a Pro Bowl in NFL history.

Jackson looking to pass during his record-breaking game in December 2019 against the Cleveland Browns

game, they lost to the Tennessee Titans. It was a hard defeat for everyone. "We just beat ourselves," Jackson said. "I had a lot of mistakes on my behalf. . . . But [Tennessee] came out to play."

Although the Ravens didn't get the results they wanted, the team looked forward to their next season. Jackson was only in his second year as an NFL quarterback. The best was still to come.

CHAPTER 3

ALMOST PERFECT

After his great performance in 2019, all eyes were on Jackson in 2020. People wanted to know if he would live up to the previous season's hype. Jackson delivered.

In his first game of the season, Jackson completed 20 of his 25 passes for 275 yards. He also led an impressive 99-yard touchdown drive, setting a new Ravens record for the longest drive in a home game. Baltimore defeated the Cleveland Browns 38–6. Jackson was on a roll. The Ravens won their second game against the Houston Texans 33–16.

Jackson during a game against the Houston Texans on September 20, 2020

The Ravens lost their next two games. But Jackson and his team returned to top form on December 8. They began a five-game winning streak. Their last game of the streak was a 38–3 win against the Cincinnati Bengals. Jackson returned to the playoffs, helping his team win their first-round game. The Ravens later lost to the Buffalo Bills.

SUPER SPORTS SCOOP

Jackson's daughter, Milan, was born on January 4, 2021. Fans don't know much about her as Jackson has kept most details private. But when she was ten months old, Jackson shared a picture on Instagram of her dressed as the character Pebbles from *The Flintstones*. His nickname for her is Lani.

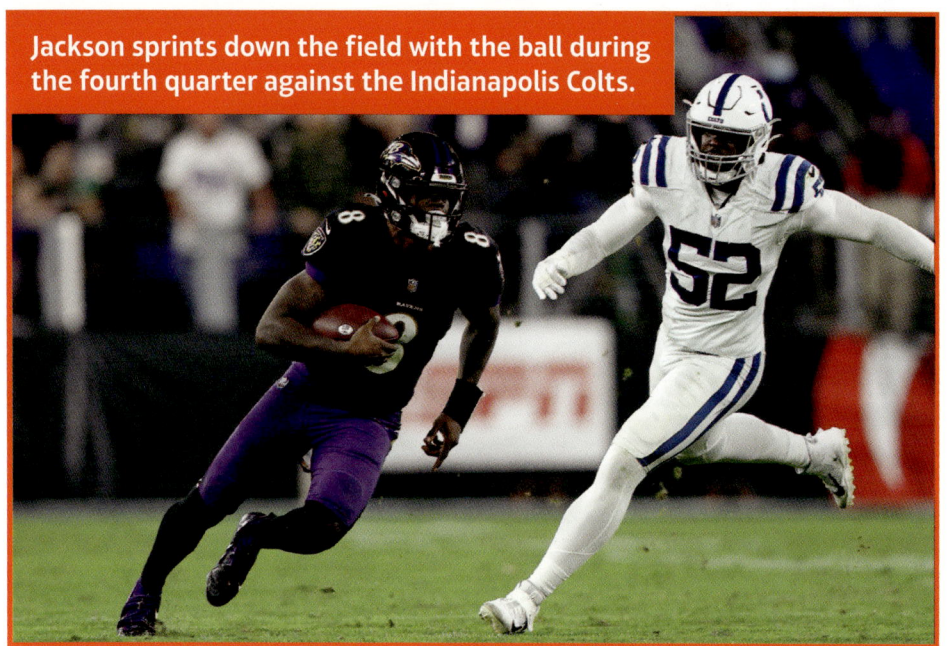

Jackson sprints down the field with the ball during the fourth quarter against the Indianapolis Colts.

Jackson was great in the next season. He threw pinpoint passes, rushed for touchdowns, and broke records. During a thrilling comeback against the Indianapolis Colts, Jackson passed for 442 yards and four touchdowns. His 442 yards in a single game was a new Baltimore Ravens record. "It was one of the greatest performances I've ever seen," Ravens head coach John Harbaugh said of Jackson after the game.

But Baltimore's luck would soon run out. On December 12, in Week 14, Jackson hurt his ankle. He missed the rest of the game and season. Without their star quarterback, Baltimore couldn't keep up and lost the rest of their games.

CHAPTER 4

MAKING HISTORY

Jackson's 2022 season with the Baltimore Ravens had some highs and lows. He had his best showing early in the season in Week 2 against the Miami Dolphins. He passed for 318 yards and three touchdowns. The team lost 42–38, but they looked in good shape to take on their next opponents.

On December 4, 2022, Jackson hurt his knee during a game against the Denver Broncos. Jackson was only supposed to sit out for three weeks. But he missed the rest of the season and did not play in the playoffs.

In a September 2022 game against the Miami Dolphins, Jackson flips into the end zone for a touchdown.

Reporters asked Jackson in 2022 if he would stay with the Ravens after his rookie contract was over. At the time, Jackson answered that he didn't know.

By 2023, Jackson had been with the Ravens for five years. He thought his skills would be better on another team, so he requested a trade. But Baltimore didn't want him to leave. They offered him a new deal. On May 4, 2023, Jackson signed a new five-year contract with the Ravens worth $260 million. This made him the highest-paid player in NFL history at the time.

Baltimore was right to value Jackson so highly. The quarterback had his best season in 2023. He ran amazing plays and rushed for touchdowns. He passed a milestone in Week 12 when he reached 5,000 career rushing yards in a game against the Los Angeles Chargers. He joined Michael Vick, Cam Newton, and Russell Wilson as the only quarterbacks in NFL history to achieve this.

Jackson (*right*) during the game against the Los Angeles Chargers when he reached 5,000 career rushing yards

On December 31, 2023, Jackson threw for 321 yards and five touchdowns with no interceptions. He recorded a perfect passer rating of 158.3 against the Miami Dolphins. "I don't know if I've seen a more impressive performance in a game," said Harbaugh.

Jackson's leadership helped the Ravens win their first division championship since 2019. His amazing showing also earned Jackson many awards, including his second

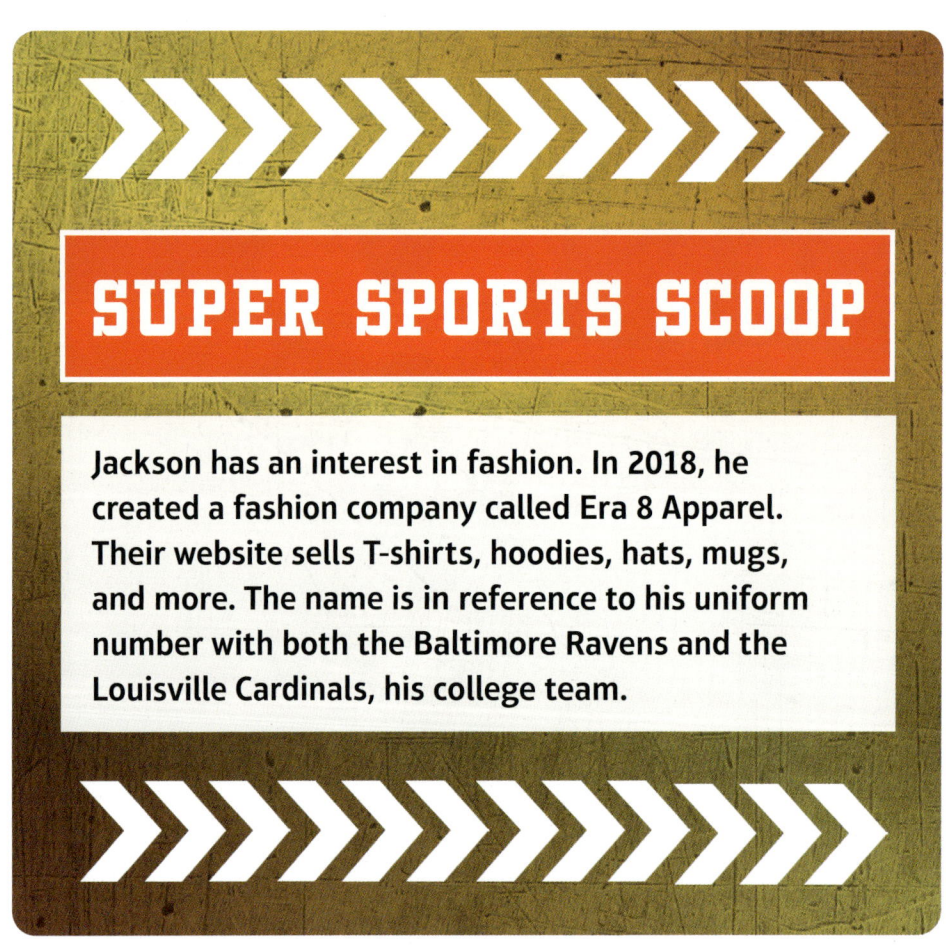

SUPER SPORTS SCOOP

Jackson has an interest in fashion. In 2018, he created a fashion company called Era 8 Apparel. Their website sells T-shirts, hoodies, hats, mugs, and more. The name is in reference to his uniform number with both the Baltimore Ravens and the Louisville Cardinals, his college team.

Jackson warming up before a game

NFL MVP award, his second First-Team All-Pro, and his third Pro Bowl.

Baltimore put up a good fight in the playoffs. They won against the Houston Texans but lost against the Kansas City Chiefs. The Chiefs went on to win the 2023 Super Bowl.

Jackson expressed his anger at losing. But he also saw it as a chance to grow. "This offseason, we're going to get right, get better, grind, and try to be in this position again," he said, "but on the other side, a victory."

LAMAR JACKSON CAREER STATS

GAMES:
86

PASSES ATTEMPTED:
2,112

PASSES COMPLETED:
1,362

PASSING TOUCHDOWNS:
125

PASSING YARDS:
15,887

RUSHING YARDS:
5,258

INTERCEPTIONS:
45

Stats are accurate through the 2023 NFL season.

GLOSSARY

contract: a legally binding agreement between two or more parties

draft: when teams take turns choosing new players

drive: a set of offensive plays

end zone: the area at each end of a football field where players score touchdowns

First-Team All-Pro: a team made up of the season's best NFL players

Heisman Trophy: an annual award given to college football's most outstanding player

hotbed: a place that favors rapid growth

interception: a pass caught by the opposing team that results in a change of possession

line of scrimmage: an imaginary line that marks the position of the ball at the start of each play

passer rating: a stat that measures how a quarterback performs at passing the ball

Pro Bowl: the NFL's all-star game

SOURCE NOTES

12 Steve Jones, "Text of Lamar Jackson's Heisman Speech," *Louisville (KY) Courier Journal*, December 10, 2016, https://www.courier-journal.com/story/sports/college/louisville/2016/12/10/full-text-lamar-jackson-heisman-speech/95289342/.

17 Jamison Hensley, "Lamar Jackson Struggles as Top-Seeded Ravens Shocked by Titans," *ESPN*, January 12, 2020, https://www.espn.com.au/nfl/story/_/id/28467215/lamar-jackson-struggles-top-seeded-ravens-shocked-titans.

21 Michael Baca, "John Harbaugh on Lamar Jackson's Comeback: 'It Was One of the Greatest Performances I've Ever Seen,'" NFL, October 12, 2021, https://www.nfl.com/news/john-harbaugh-on-lamar-jackson-s-comeback-it-was-one-of-the-greatest-performance.

26 Jamison Hensley, "Lamar Jackson Records Perfect Rating as Ravens Win AFC North," *ESPN*, December 31, 2023, https://www.espn.com/nfl/story/_/id/39217864/lamar-jackson-records-perfect-rating-ravens-win-afc-north.

27 Kevin Patra, "Ravens QB Lamar Jackson 'Not Frustrated' but 'Angry' about Loss to Chiefs in AFC Championship Game," NFL, January 29, 2024, https://www.nfl.com/news/ravens-qb-lamar-jackson-not-frustrated-but-angry-about-loss-to-chiefs-in-afc-championship-game.

LEARN MORE

Britannica Kids: Baltimore Ravens
https://kids.britannica.com/students/article/Baltimore-Ravens/571000

Coleman, Ted. *Baltimore Ravens*. Mendota Heights, MN: Press Box Books, 2022.

Goodman, Michael E. *Baltimore Ravens*. Mankato, MN: Creative Company, 2023.

Kiddle: Baltimore Ravens Facts for Kids
https://kids.kiddle.co/Baltimore_Ravens

Kiddle: Lamar Jackson Facts for Kids
https://kids.kiddle.co/Lamar_Jackson

Lowe, Alexander. *G.O.A.T. Football Quarterbacks*. Minneapolis: Lerner Publications, 2023.

INDEX

Agholor, Nelson, 5–6

Detroit Lions, 4–6
draft, 5, 12–13

Flacco, Joe, 14–15

Heisman Trophy, 5, 12

Kansas City Chiefs, 27

Louisville Cardinals, 11, 26

MVP, 5, 7, 14, 16, 27

perfect passer rating, 26
Pro Bowl, 16, 27

streak, 20

touchdown, 5–6, 10, 12, 19, 21–22, 25–26
trade, 24

University of Louisville, 11–12

PHOTO ACKNOWLEDGMENTS

Image credits: Perry Knotts via AP, p. 4; Michael Owens/Getty Images, p. 6; AP Photo/Alex Brandon, p. 7; Jim Rassol/South Florida Sun Sentinel/Tribune News Service via Getty Images, p. 8; Rich Graessle/Icon Sportswire via Getty Images, p. 9; Madeline Gray/The Palm Beach Post/ZUMAPRESS.com/Alamy Live News, p. 10; Kevin C. Cox/Getty Images, p. 11; Tim Warner/Getty Images, p. 13; Rob Leiter/Getty Images, p. 14; Patrick Smith/Getty Images, pp. 15, 21, 22; AP Photo/Ron Schwane, p. 17; Mark Goldman/Icon Sportswire via Getty Images, p. 18; Bob Levey/Getty Images, p. 19; Rob Carr/Getty Images, p. 23; Kim Hairston/Baltimore Sun/Tribune News Service via Getty Images, p. 24; Jevone Moore/Icon Sportswire via Getty Images, p. 25; Michael Owens/Getty Images, p. 27.

Cover: AP Photo/Nick Wass.